Major League SOCCER

Minnesota United FC

Kaitlyn Duling

Copyright © 2020 by Mitchell Lane Publishers. All rights reserved. No part of this book may be reproduced without written permission from the publisher. Printed and bound in the United States of America.

Printing 1 2 3 4 5 6 7 8

First Edition, 2020.
Author: Kaitlyn Duling
Designer: Ed Morgan
Editor: Lisa Petrillo

Series: Major League Soccer
Title: Minnesota United FC / by Kaitlyn Duling

Hallandale, FL : Mitchell Lane Publishers, [2020]

Library bound ISBN: 9781680204889
eBook ISBN: 9781680204896

PHOTO CREDITS: Design Elements, freepik.com, Getty Images, p. 12 and 17 andywitchger CC-BY-SA-2.0

Contents

Words in **bold** throughout can be found in the Glossary.

When you step into a soccer **stadium**, you can hear the roar of the crowd. You can smell the snacks. You see the ball zooming across the field. There is nothing like it! Soccer is played all across the globe. The game is played in backyards. It is played on school playgrounds. It is even played indoors. It is the world's most popular sport. Some players will make it to the top of professional soccer. In the United States, the top league is Major League Soccer.

Major League Soccer is the newest pro soccer league in North America. Before MLS, there were other leagues. They were not quite as popular. Football is played in the NFL. Baseball is played in the MLB. Basketball has the NBA. Now soccer has its own top league. Teams began playing in the MLS in 1996. At first, there were just ten teams. It grew very slowly.

In the last few years, soccer has become more popular in North America. Ever since the 2002 FIFA World Cup, **fans** have been extra excited about Major League Soccer (MLS). More teams were added in the mid-2000s. This brought the MLS to a total of 23 teams. Twenty teams play in the U.S. Three teams play in Canada.

Each year, MLS teams play their regular season. This lasts from March to October. They play matches against other MLS teams. During this regular season, each of the teams plays a total of 34 matches. The teams are divided into two **conferences**: East and West. The Eastern Conference includes eleven teams located east of Illinois. D.C. United and New England Revolution are two of the best teams in the East. The Western Conference has twelve of its own teams. The Western Conference stretches from Minnesota to the Pacific Ocean. The L.A. Galaxy has won eight Western Conference titles. That's the most in the conference.

Team History

Minnesota United FC is a Major League Soccer club. The team is based in Minneapolis-Saint Paul, Minnesota. Minnesota is in the northern United States. Minneapolis and Saint Paul are two "Twin Cities." They are located right next to each other. Saint Paul is the capital of Minnesota. Minneapolis is the largest city. About 700,000 people live in the area. Minnesota United is a new team. It started in 2017. This team was the 22nd club in the MLS. It plays in the Western Conference.

MLS has grown a few times. The soccer commissioner is in charge of announcing the new teams and cities. The Minnesota team was announced in the spring of 2015. It is owned by a group of people. They are led by businessman Dr. Bill McGuire. Many fans were excited. It is fun to have a team in your home state!

Carlos Alberto (*left*) of the New York Cosmos takes on Ricardo Alonso of the Minnesota Kicks in January 1980.

Though this is Minnesota's first MLS franchise, the state has a long soccer history. Its first pro soccer team was the Minnesota Kicks. The Kicks were part of the North American Soccer League (NASL). The team played from 1976 to 1981. An **amateur** team, the Minnesota Thunder, began in 1990. It lasted for 18 years before closing down. Finally, a team with the name Minnesota United FC was first introduced to the Twin Cities in 2010 as NSC Minnesota. It would later be known as Minnesota Stars FC. The team played in the NASL, a league that ended. That team would be the seed of what would become MLS Minnesota United FC.

Each team has unique colors, logos, and uniforms. Minnesota United FC has gray, black, bright red, and light blue. Gray represents the state's rich deposits of iron. The blue stripe featured on the team's **crest** stands for the Mississippi River, the mighty river that runs along the state's western edge. The team has its own crest. The crest itself has a light gray background, blue stripe, and a large black loon. The loon is the state bird of Minnesota. It has a bright red eye. Its wings feature eleven feathers. There is one feather for each player on the soccer pitch or field.

Even the font or style of the words on the crest is unique to the state. It was created by a factory in Minneapolis.

Each year, MLS teams unveil new uniforms. In soccer, a uniform is also known as a **kit**. The 2018 Minnesota United kit features light and dark gray stripes. It comes in long sleeve, short sleeve, and a slightly different design for away games. The goalie wears a bright blue kit.

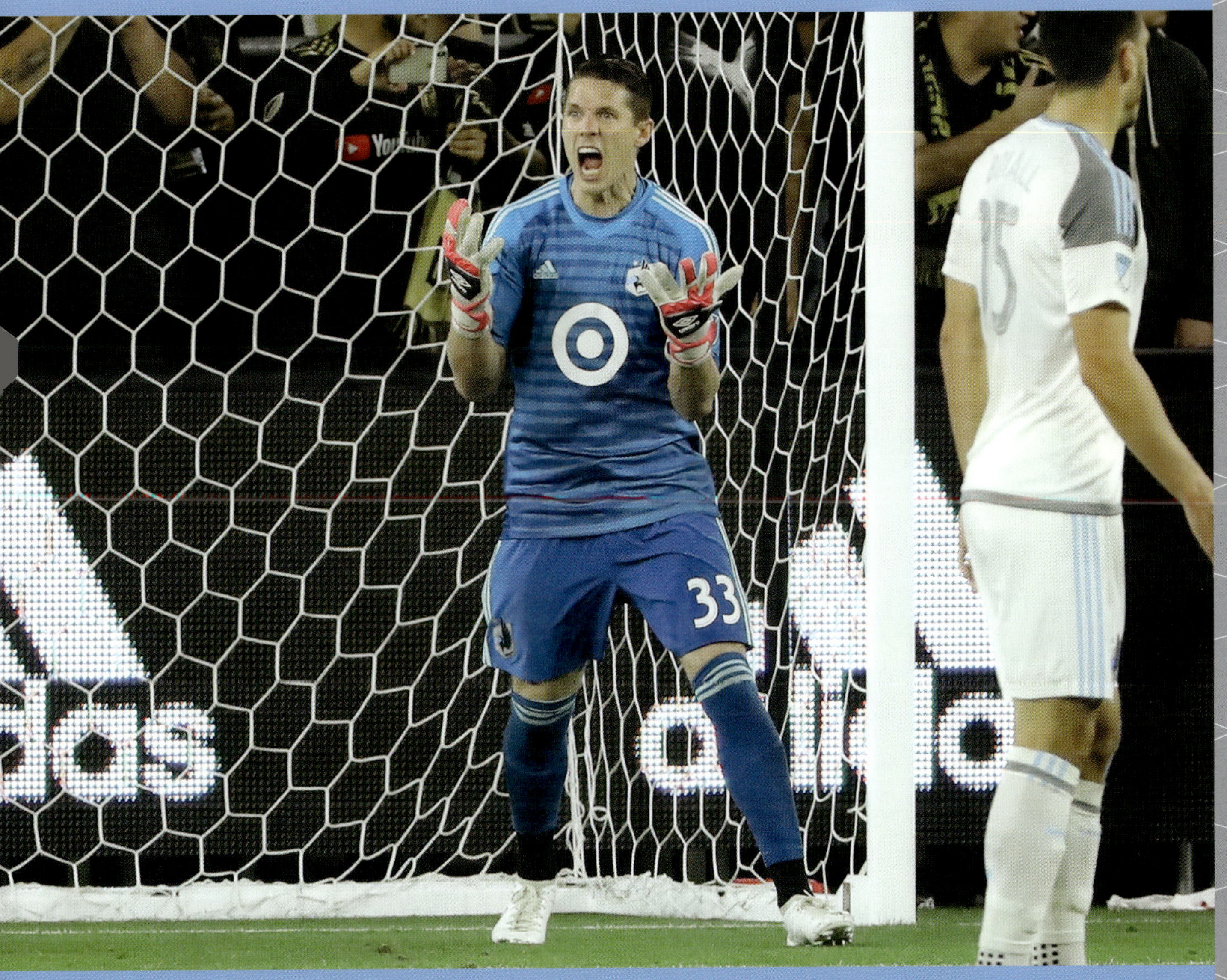

Goalkeeper Bobby Shuttleworth (*left*) and Michael Boxall in May 2018

Chapter Two

When the team started in 2015, plans for a new soccer field were just getting started. Since 2017, Minnesota United FC has played at TCF Bank Stadium, which is home to the University of Minnesota football team. The stadium is on the school's campus. It was built in 2009 and holds 50,805 seats.

Since 2015, the "true" home of the Minnesota United FC has been under construction. The new stadium is known as Allianz Field and it is planned to open in March 2019. It will be located in Saint Paul. The stadium will only host soccer games. It will hold almost 20,000 fans. The field will be all-natural grass instead of artificial turf. Players like grass better because turf gets dangerous when wet and slippery. The outdoor field will offer a more cozy setting.

A spectacular move by Minnesota's Abu Danladi (*left*) against Jack Elliott of the Philadelphia Union thrills fans at TCT Bank Stadium in September 2017.

This young team hasn't yet set any impressive records. The players did not qualify for the playoffs in 2017 or 2018. They ended the 2017 season in ninth place. The next year, they were tenth in the Western Conference. But the team has an impressive roster of passionate players! Darwin Quintero is the second top player. He scored eleven goals during his first season with the team in 2018. Christian Ramirez was Minnesota's top-scorer, with 21 goals since 2017. Ramirez now plays for the Los Angeles FC, the newest team in the League.

Throughout the team's history, it has had only one head coach—Adrian Heath. He grew up playing in his home country of England. Heath has been coaching the U.S. since 2008, when he started with the Austin Azteks. The team also has several assistant coaches on staff. They keep three goalkeepers (goalies) in rotation to take turns in the tough position.

Fun Facts

1. **The "FC" in the team name stands for "football club." In Europe and South America, the sport of soccer is called "football."**
2. **Minnesota United FC supporters have given their team a nickname: the Loons.**
3. **Building Allianz Field may cost about $140 million.**

Playing Our Game

Soccer is called football in many other countries outside the United States. It has long been the world's most popular sport. Around the world, more than four out of ten people consider themselves soccer fans. That's a lot of fans!

But in the United States, American football has long had the most fans. **Professional** basketball and baseball also have huge fan bases. This means that soccer and MLS have been fighting an uphill battle to win more fans. But it's getting easier each year. International soccer stars have made the sport more popular. An increase in televised games has made it easier to see on cable stations and the internet.

Goalkeeper(GK)
Right back defender (RB)
Left back defender (LB)
Center back defender (CB)
Left midfielder (LM)
Center midfielder (CM)
Right midfielder (RM)
Left forward (LF)
Right forward (RF)

Soccer is simple and easy-to-follow—if you can keep up! It is a fast-paced game. Each team is made up of 11 players. Both teams have their own goals at one end of the "pitch" or field. The field is divided into two halves. There are marks on the field for the halfway point, penalty areas, corners, and the center. The game begins inside the center circle. The field is made out of grass or artificial turf. It is always green.

There are just four positions in soccer. Goalkeepers defend their team's goal. Defenders try to keep the other team from scoring. Forwards are in charge of scoring goals. They kick the soccer ball into the goal. Midfielders spend most of their time running. They do a little defending and a little attacking. Each soccer game has at least one **referee**. The referee watches the game from the field. Referees enforce the rules. He or she makes sure the game is fun, fair, and safe for everyone.

Chapter Three

During a soccer game, players try to move the soccer ball into the goal. It sounds similar to basketball or American football, but with one key difference. Soccer players may not use their hands! They use their feet, legs, and heads to move the ball. To control the ball, players **dribble** with their feet as they move down the pitch. They might pass the ball back and forth between teammates. When a player decides to try for a goal, he or she "shoots" the ball into the net. The goalie will try to block the ball. When it flies past the goalie and into the net, the team has won a goal! The team with the most goals at the end is the winner.

Soccer might be easy to understand, but it isn't easy to play. Soccer players use their legs, hips, backs, and the tops of their heads to try to win games. Each MLS match is broken into two 45-minute halves. Teams break for 15 minutes in-between. An entire MLS match takes about two hours.

Minnesota United FC fans are passionate about their team and their state. The oldest, proudest supporters of the team call themselves the Dark Clouds. It is said that wherever Minnesota United FC goes, the Dark Clouds follow! They have been supporting professional soccer in the state since 2004. Another cheering squad, the True North Elite, are more intense. They are known for being loud and proud. Because the team is so new, it doesn't yet have any major rivals. Fans cheer on Minnesota United FC no matter who they are playing.

Minnesota United FC True North Elite fans

The "United" in the team's name comes from the desire to unite the cities of Saint Paul and Minneapolis around their shared soccer team. Minnesota United FC is also known as MNUFC and the Loons. The team has its own mascot. He is a silly loon named PK who likes to search for adventures. He's not the best soccer player. PK gets the fans excited about their team. No one is quite sure where the name "PK" came from, but it has stuck.

Fun Facts

1. **Prior to kickoff at Minnesota United games, a loon call is played over the loudspeakers.**
2. **A third Minnesota soccer supporters' group, Wolf's Head, was formed in 2014.**
3. **The earliest soccer games were probably played in ancient China and Japan.**

Our Best Players

Minnesota United FC has a full roster of young talent. As teammates they are just beginning to bond. Though each game only features eleven players, there are around 30 players on the roster with most of them waiting on the sidelines. There is some player movement in soccer. Athletes get traded and loaned to other teams. A player who may begin his career in California might find himself in Chicago for the next season! Roster changes are exciting to watch. Minnesota is especially interesting. The team is just getting started. There is a full slate of future stars ready to make a big impression.

Darwin Quintero

Star Forward

The newest and most talked-about player on the Minnesota team is Darwin Quintero. He is the first Designated Player in the team's short history. Each MLS team is allowed up to three Designated Players. These players make more money than their teammates. This helps Major League Soccer compete for top international players. Quintero is from Tumaco, Colombia, and he joined Minnesota United in spring 2018. He became a professional player in 2005. He played for Deportes Tolima and the Colombian national team. He then became a star in Mexican soccer, playing for Club Santos Laguna. In Mexico, he became a well-known forward. He is the top goal-scorer on Minnesota. In 2018, he topped the statistics lists with the most goals, assists, and shots on his team. Minnesota United fans can't wait to follow his success in the coming years.

Chapter Four

Kevin Molino

Midfielder

Midfielder Kevin Molino was a star during the 2017 regular season. He just keeps getting better! The talented attacker grew up in Trinidad and Tobago. While living there, he played in the Pan-American Games, Caribbean Cup, and Gold Cup. His pro career took him to the United Soccer League. This was another professional soccer league based in the U.S. and Canada. He played for Orlando City in the USL. He then followed the team as it transitioned to Major League Soccer. In January 2017, Molino was traded to Minnesota United FC from Orlando City. In 2017, he made seven goals for Minnesota United. In 2018, he scored two goals early in the season. Sadly, an injury forced Molino to miss the rest of the season. Fans are hoping he'll be back and better than ever in 2019!

United States versus Belgium at the 1930 FIFA World Cup. US won 3-0.

Argentina versus Uruguay

Fun Facts

1. The first FIFA World Cup was played in 1930.
2. The first Women's World Cup wasn't held until 1991, 61 years after the association competition began.
3. A traditional soccer ball has 32 panels, each representing a country in Europe.

Soccer Across the Globe

Soccer is the most popular sport on Earth. It has more TV viewers than any other sport. It is played in more than 200 countries. It has been popular in Europe for a long time. South American countries have long loved soccer too. Many nations have their own pro leagues and national teams. National teams represent them in tournaments. National teams play in the Olympics. But players don't just play in their own countries. Many travel thousands of miles to play on pro teams. All of the current Major League Soccer teams include players from outside of the United States and Canada.

When MLS teams are forming their rosters, they must keep many rules in mind. One important part of building a roster is counting the international roster slots. MLS only allows a certain number of international players to play in the League each year. There are a total of 184 slots divided among the 23 soccer clubs. Clubs can trade the slots, so some teams end up with more than eight international players. Others have even fewer. The rest of the roster is filled with players from the United States. Canadian teams can use U.S. or Canadian players to fill their domestic slots. During the 2018 season, FC Dallas had the largest number of international players. They had twelve. It is easier to find great players when you can search all across the globe.

Chapter Five

During the 2018 season, Minnesota United FC had ten players from outside the U.S. Several came from soccer powerhouses Colombia and Brazil. These countries are in South America. Countries as far away as Ghana, Peru, Finland, and Cameroon were also represented. When it was founded in the early 1990s, one goal of MLS was to develop talented American players. It also hoped to boost American interest in soccer. These days, though, the League is going global. In order to grow and bring in profits, MLS has had to look across the globe for the best players.

While other professional sports have diverse rosters, soccer is one of the most international. How do the players overcome barriers like communication and culture? Luckily, soccer requires very little talking. Players can signal to each other using their hands, bodies, and sounds. And even though players move to the U.S. to play for MLS, they still use scheduled breaks to travel and play for their home teams. That way, talented athletes can represent both their club and their country. It's a win-win!

Soccer has long been a popular sport. European and South American pro leagues create soccer celebrities. In the U.S., it has taken awhile for soccer to take off in popularity. With the help of the MLS, it is starting to happen. Young people in Minnesota are growing up with a pro team. They can be proud of their team. They can become fans. They might even be inspired to try soccer for themselves. Minnesota United FC is new, but it will probably stick around for a long time.

Fun Facts

1. The first big-name international star who joined MLS was David Beckham of England.
2. The highest-paid player in MLS history is a Brazilian footballer named Kaká. His final season with Orlando City ended in 2017.

What You **Should Know**

- Modern soccer began in England around 1830.
- Most countries call the game football except the U.S., Canada, Japan, and Korea.
- Early MLS teams had nouns in their names like the L.A. Galaxy and the Dallas Burn. Today teams like Minnesota United FC reminds fans of popular European teams like Manchester United.
- Minnesota United FC plays in Minneapolis-Saint Paul, Minnesota.
- 2017 was the first year of play.
- The team is managed by Adrian Heath.
- They play at Allianz Field.
- PK the Loon is the team mascot.
- The team is young and diverse.

Quick Stats

2018 regular season

Squad Size: 30

Ranked: 10th in the Western Conference

2018 Regular Season Wins: 12

Percent International: 50%

Average Player Age: 27

Average Attendance: 23,902 people

Largest Attendance: 52,242 people

Longest Winning Streak: 3 matches

Top Goal-Scorer: Darwin Quintero

Most Assists: Darwin Quintero

Minnesota **Timeline**

2015 MLS announces Minnesota United as the league's newest club.

2016 It is announced that Minnesota United will play its first seasons in TCF Bank Stadium, home to the University of Minnesota Golden Gophers.

2016 Former soccer player Adrian Heath signs on as Minnesota United's manager.

2017 March: Minnesota United plays and loses its first-ever match, 1-5.

July: Allianz Field is announced as the name of the team's new stadium.

January: Target becomes Minnesota United's first official kit sponsor.

2018 March: Dominic Quintero joins the team as Minnesota's first Designated Player.

July: Minnesota United FC wins against Saprissa, a Costa Rican pro team.

August: The team loses its top scorer Christian Ramirez in a trade to Los Angeles FC.

October: Minnesota United plays its final game in TCF Bank Stadium.

Glossary

amateur
A sport in which players are not paid for their time or performance

conference
A group of sports teams that play one another

crest
A design that represents a family or group

dribble
To control a ball with your feet, moving it around opponents and obstacles

fans
Those who have a great deal of devotion and enthusiasm for a person, organization, or team

FIFA
The international governing body of soccer

kit
Soccer uniform

professional
Sports in which athletes are paid for their time and performance

referee
A person who watches a match to make sure the rules are followed appropriately

roster
List of players on a team

stadium
A large building, usually roofless, with tiered seats meant for spectators

Further Reading

Latham, Andrew. *Soccer Smarts for Kids: 60 Skills, Strategies, and Secrets.* Berkeley, CA: Rockridge Press, 2016.

McCabe, Matthew. *It's Great to Be a Fan in Minnesota* (Focus Readers). Mendota Heights, MN: North Star Editions, 2018.

Savage, Jeff. *Soccer Super Stats.* New York City, NY: Lerner Publishing, 2017.

Zweig, Eric. *Absolute Expert: Soccer.* Washington, DC: National Geographic Kids, 2018.

On the Internet

DK Find Out! Soccer
https://www.dkfindout.com/us/sports/soccer/

Major League Soccer
https://www.mlssoccer.com/

Scholastic News: The World of Soccer
http://teacher.scholastic.com/scholasticnews/indepth/soccer2005/soccerstories/index.asp?article=soccerhome&topic=0

Sports Illustrated Kids: Soccer
https://www.sikids.com/soccer

Index

About the Author

Kaitlyn Duling believes in the power of words to change hearts, minds, and, ultimately, actions. An avid reader and writer who grew up in Illinois, she now resides in Washington, DC. She loves to learn about all kinds of sports. Kaitlyn likes to run marathons, but stays in the fan section when it comes to soccer! You can learn more about her at www.kaitlynduling.com.